This bite-sized book ~~~~~
light and useful ~~~~~
learning. It will h~

- Understand ~~~~~
learner
- Appreciate th~~~~~~~~~~~~~~~~ ...wellbeing
- Be open-mind~~~~ ...ultivate a growth mindset
- Motivate yourself to want to learn and grow
- Take personal action and turn knowledge into
wisdom

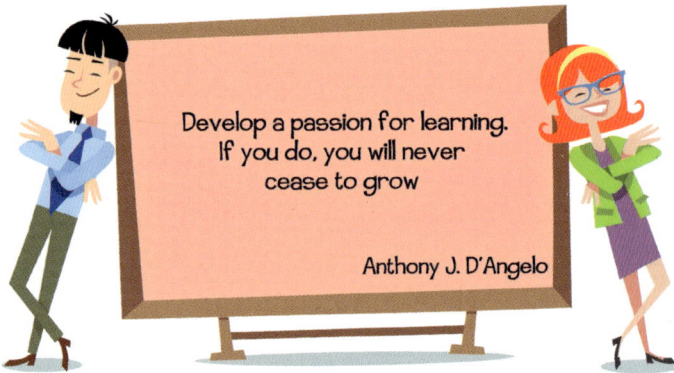

Develop a passion for learning.
If you do, you will never
cease to grow

Anthony J. D'Angelo

Learn and grow

We are all people in progress and one of the most exciting things about being alive is that we never stop learning and we never stop growing. Seeking out opportunities for continuous learning supports both our personal and professional development and enriches our lives.

Learning can be enlightening, stimulating, fun and it is also great for our overall wellbeing.

Anyone who stops learning is old, whether at twenty or eighty. Anyone who keeps learning stays young

Henry Ford

What is lifelong learning?

Lifelong learning is the continual, voluntary and self-directed pursuit of knowledge and skills for our own development. This type of learning may well take place outside of a formal educational institute such as school, university or corporate training.

Lifelong learning embraces both formal and informal learning opportunities and enhances our understanding of the world around us. Being a lifelong learner can of course mean different things to different people, however at its core, it's about cultivating curiosity and satisfying our thirst for knowledge and wisdom.

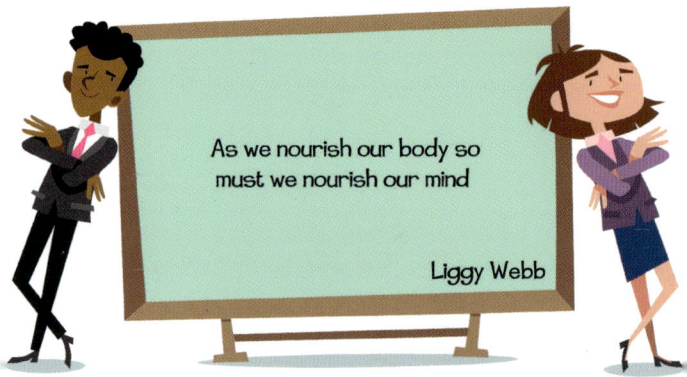

As we nourish our body so
must we nourish our mind

Liggy Webb

Learning and wellbeing

Continuous learning throughout our lives can improve life-satisfaction, optimism and self-confidence. The urge to explore and seek out new things helps us to remain vigilant and gain knowledge about our constantly changing environment. This may explain why our brains have evolved to release dopamine and other feel-good chemicals when we encounter new things.

Learning and developing new skills can also help to keep our brain strong and healthy which is especially beneficial as we get older.

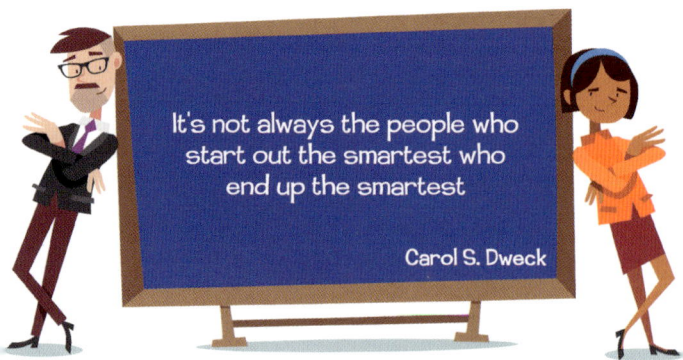

It's not always the people who start out the smartest who end up the smartest

Carol S. Dweck

Growth and fixed mindset

A fixed mindset is where we believe that our basic abilities, intelligence and talents are fixed traits, and we then focus on reproducing what we already know and do. With this mindset we can become rigid in our thinking and focus on seeking perfection and avoid the risk of failure.

With a growth mindset we understand that our talents and abilities can be developed through continual learning, effort and persistence. Stanford University psychologist Carol Dweck, through decades of research on achievement and success, has pioneered the term growth mindset and her work and books are well worth exploring.

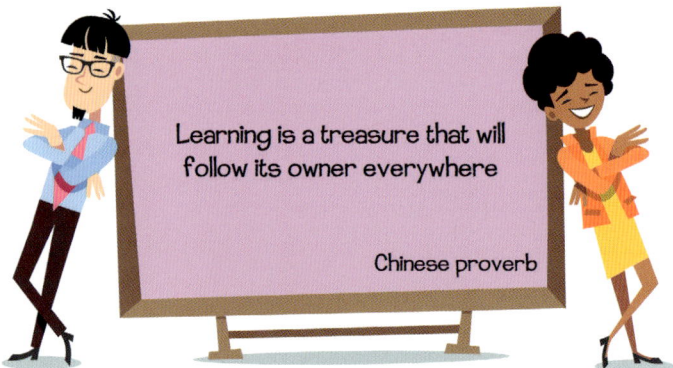

Learning is a treasure that will follow its owner everywhere

Chinese proverb

Examples of lifelong learning

There are many ways that we can cultivate lifelong learning and here are a few examples:

- ✓ Challenge yourself and step out of your comfort zone
- ✓ Learn to use new pieces of technology
- ✓ Listen to a podcast or watch a TED talk
- ✓ Embrace opportunities to upskill during employment
- ✓ Join a social club and meet new people
- ✓ Learn a new language or musical instrument
- ✓ Take up a new hobby or learn a new skill
- ✓ Do some crossword and sudoko puzzles
- ✓ Start a conversation with someone you haven't met before
- ✓ Play a new game or learn a new sport
- ✓ Ask others for examples of what they do to keep learning

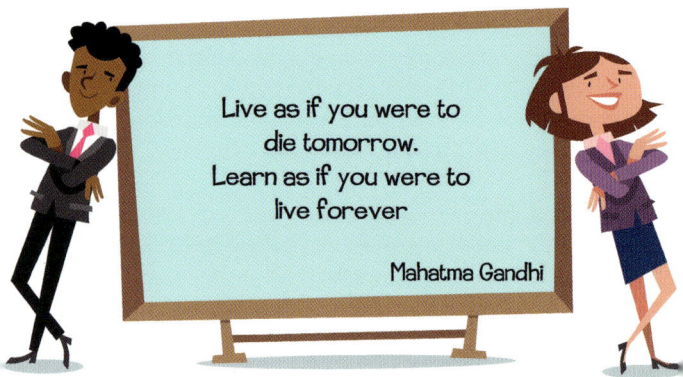

Live as if you were to die tomorrow.
Learn as if you were to live forever

Mahatma Gandhi

Learning styles

There is no right way of learning because we are all different and we all learn in a variety of ways. However, identifying and understanding our own unique learning style can make a big difference to how we learn best and at what speed.

Learning styles essentially are about our preferred way of absorbing, processing, comprehending and retaining information. The four key learning styles are often referred to as visual, auditory, tactile and kinaesthetic, however there are multiple models around learning styles that are well worth exploring.

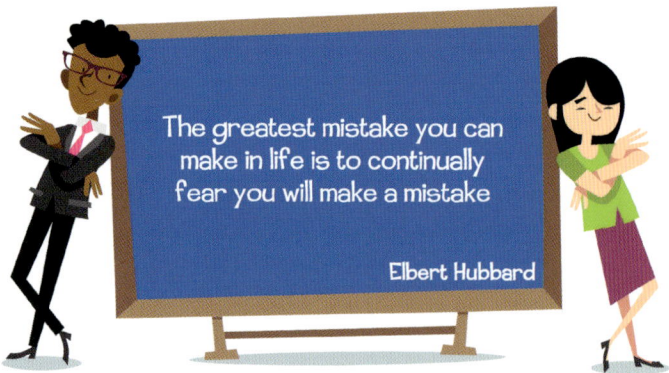

The greatest mistake you can make in life is to continually fear you will make a mistake

Elbert Hubbard

Fear of failure and excuses

"I'm not ready", "I'm too old", "I'm not good enough", "I'll probably fail anyway". These are all examples of excuses we can make, and these self-limiting beliefs will only sabotage our ability to grow.

Fear of failure and making a mistake can be one of the greatest obstacles to taking on new challenges, however every new experience is a learning opportunity and the gateway to personal development and growth. When we take the view that there are no mistakes in life, only lessons, then we will liberate ourselves and be more open to lifelong learning.

Lifelong learning

Lifelong learning can be about the gradual changes that we make and being more conscious of how we spend our time. We may decide to listen to an educational podcast rather than scrolling aimlessly through social media, or watch an interesting and enlightening documentary instead of a sitcom we have seen before.

Over time, micro-changes become macro-habits, and this can help us to cultivate a learning mindset.

The next few pages will share some suggestions on ways that we can become lifelong learners to keep learning and growing ...

How to embrace lifelong learning

In the beginner's mind there are many possibilities, but in the expert's there are few

Shunryu Suzuki

Refresh your thinking

Embracing a beginner's mindset refers to having an attitude of openness, eagerness and lack of preconceptions. The term is translated from the word, Shoshin, which comes from Zen Buddhism. By adopting a beginner's mindset we approach every situation we encounter as if it is the first time we are experiencing it.

It helps us to be free of preconceptions of how something works and free of expectations about what will happen next. A beginner's mindset helps us to be curious about understanding things more deeply and more open to a world of possibilities and fresh thinking.

Learn to enjoy and respect
each other's differences

Fred Meijer

Expand your world view

Our world view is a framework of beliefs, values and attitudes which affects everything we perceive, think, feel and do. As we evolve we can become restricted by the boundaries of what we experience, so constantly expanding our world view will help us to be more open to new experiences and learning.

Reading things that we don't necessarily agree with or instigating conversations with people who challenge our perspective is a good place to start. Expanding our horizons by embracing new experiences will also help us to develop as well-rounded, balanced and inclusive human beings. By keeping an open mind and open heart we will be able to constantly learn and grow.

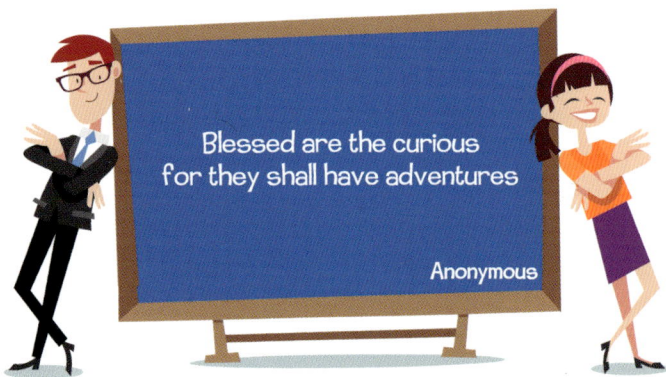

Blessed are the curious
for they shall have adventures

Anonymous

Be curious

When we seek out challenges and new experiences, we broaden our horizons. It is the major ingredient of learning and life is never boring for a curious person. Curiosity and exploration can help us to embark on some of our greatest adventures. It is the first step our mind takes toward our most valuable discoveries.

Learning something new, overcoming challenges and exploring our potential are all possible because we are curious, and we have the desire and courage to explore.

When you talk, you are only repeating what you already know.

But if you listen, you may learn something new

Dalai Lama

Listen and learn

Listening is one of the most powerful ways that we can learn. When we practise active listening, we focus on what someone else is saying rather than listening to the narrative that is going on in our own head. By being present and seeking to understand what the other person is saying without making assumptions and judgments can help us to absorb all the information that is being shared.

Everyone we meet knows something that we don't and finding everyone we meet interesting is a great place to start. You never know what you will learn!

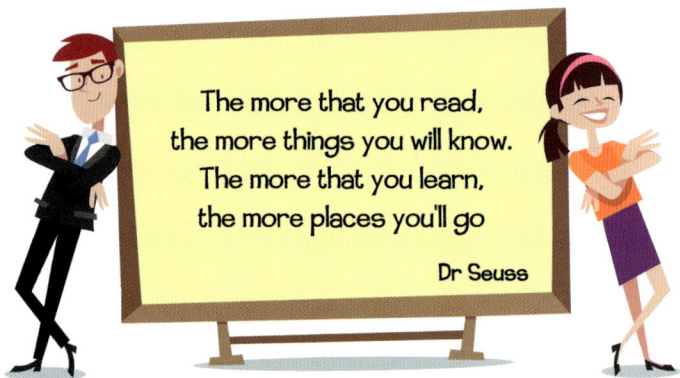

The more that you read,
the more things you will know.
The more that you learn,
the more places you'll go

Dr Seuss

Read books

Books have the capacity to revolutionise our lives. They help us to gain new information, insights and perspectives, learn about other people's experiences, as well as expand our ideas and ambitions.

There are many benefits to reading as it has been scientifically proven to reduce stress, improve concentration and memory, strengthen our writing abilities and boost our creativity. Reading is key to adult education and supporting lifelong learning.

Embrace technology

Technology is advancing all the time and can provide us with some fun opportunities to practise what we learn as well as easy-to-access information on any subject we are interested in.

There is a wealth of online resources out there that will help us to learn. Whether it is listening to podcasts, downloading e-books, embarking on some distance-learning courses or joining forums, the possibilities are endless. Being as technically savvy as we can be will also help us to keep up-to-date with all the new innovations and opportunities that are available to us as lifelong learners.

Manage your time well

Life in the "busy ages" is a constant bombardment of information and overwhelming choice, which can lead to feelings of overstimulation and agitation. Taking time out to stop and reflect on what is making us busy is a great place to start.

Great time management skills will help us to feel more in control of our energy levels and establish a better life balance. By managing our time well we will be able to create more space and opportunity to learn new things and focus on our personal development. Scheduling time in for learning as part of our daily plan is a great place to start.

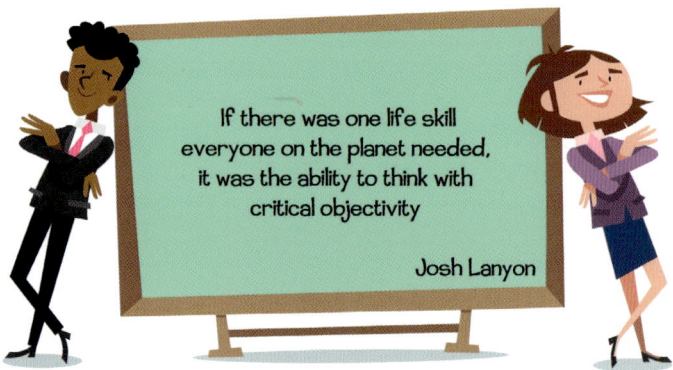

If there was one life skill
everyone on the planet needed,
it was the ability to think with
critical objectivity

Josh Lanyon

Apply critical thinking skills

Critical thinking is the process of analysing, evaluating and rationalising information objectively. This helps us to draw conclusions from a set of information and discriminate between what is useful and what is not.

It is a way of thinking in which we don't just accept everything we are exposed to at face value. Critical thinking is about taking on board an approach that will help us to rigorously question and challenge information. This, in turn, will improve the quality of our learning.

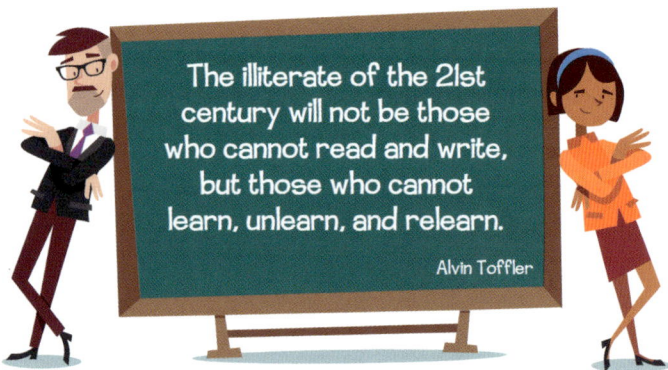

The illiterate of the 21st century will not be those who cannot read and write, but those who cannot learn, unlearn, and relearn.

Alvin Toffler

Learn to unlearn and relearn

In a rapidly changing world continuous learning alone is not enough and our ability to unlearn and relearn is just as important. Continually evaluating and challenging knowledge to ensure what we learn is relevant and up-to-date is essential.

Unlearning is a process and starts with the acknowledgement that something we have learnt earlier is now incorrect or obsolete. We then need to erase the conditioning and misconceptions from our mind for good and relearn different information and behaviours. This can be challenging and requires effort, patience and persistence.

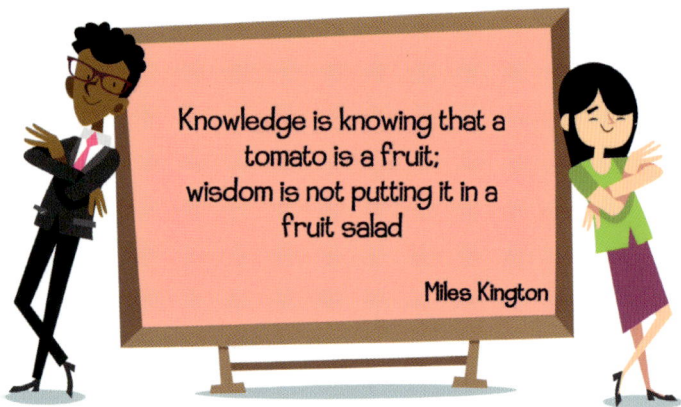

Knowledge is knowing that a tomato is a fruit;
wisdom is not putting it in a fruit salad

Miles Kington

Learning and wisdom

Wisdom is the ability to contemplate and take action by applying knowledge, experience, understanding, common sense and insight.

The ability to learn and to actively do something constructive and beneficial with what we have learnt is the real wisdom. By embracing lifelong learning, we will never stop growing and as we live and learn we have the capacity to become wiser and more enlightened and fulfilled.

Happy lifelong learning ☺

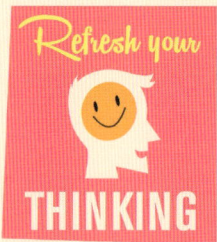